THE EGO

AND THE

CENTAUR

Jean Garrigue

THE EGO

AND THE

CENTAUR

GREENWOOD PRESS, PUBLISHERS
WESTPORT, CONNECTICUT

The Library of Congress has catalogued this publication as follows:

Library of Congress Cataloging in Publication Data

Garrigue, Jean, 1912–
    The ego and the centaur.

    Poems.
    I. Title.
    ₍PS3513.A7217E4 1972₎   811'.5'4   76-138236
    ISBN 0-8371-5593-2

Acknowledgment

Some of these poems were first published in *Horizon,
The Partisan Review, Accent, The Kenyon Review, The
Sewanee Review,* and *The Quarterly Review, The New
Republic, Poetry, Chimera, Common Sense,* and in the
anthologies: *Cross Section 1943, New Poems 1942
and 1943, Five Young American Poets 1944*
and *New Directions 1946.*

Copyright 1947 by New Directions

Originally published in 1947
by New Directions, New York

Reprinted with the permission
of Jean Garrigue

First Greenwood Reprinting 1972

Library of Congress Catalogue Card Number 76-138236

ISBN 0-8371-5593-2

Printed in the United States of America

for

ELIZABETH BRAYTON

Contents

I

LOOKING GLASS AND

ELEGY

The Soldiers, the Birds and the Monuments

ALL SAUNTER in the park past ponds and rinks
This outdoor, shirt-sleeve holiday.
So hatless and with treats to give
(Thus beasts pull tricks to nudge their charmed elders)
All smile or stare their liberty away
Like children wavering 'twixt distracting wonders.
Leaves fall and flag and dye the trampled ground
Where statues with commodious brow, the out-
Stretched hand, deign with the civic poise
Though pigeons weight and interrupt that pose.

Far-off a bell is battering massive time
And picaresquely scoring 'gainst us all
Our careless ease beneath the day,
In love with love and sociability.
All wander 'mid the five-cent stands
And spectacles of tunnels, ponds and rinks
With slow surprise, as if to seize
The spaces of full-hearted emptiness,
As if a geniused trident lurked above
To prove the briny spurs and flowers and drugs
Of that mad, pondered, rainy coil beneath.

The leaves, three-quarter discourse of the year,
Fall moodily, with unmethodical pleasure,
According to a wind I cannot feel
Or solaced by some subtler law.
Perhaps the far-off bell now scatters them
To solemnize the Roman summer's rout.

13

While then I note beneath the black swan wing
White feathers lining it, and on
The pelican's head a fine-frond crown,
His pride's top-notch, though when he swims
He's no more graceful than he is waddling.
He is too big! Though his wing-spread dazes
And fills the heart, what does he do but quill
For oil or mighty fleas? (with his cracking bill.)
O empty cages where late herons stood,
Permit me candor of an excited world!

But then, quick down the promenade the soldiers come.
Their shouts in rank are rancorous with drill.
Pigeons, affronted, in a drunken rush
Rise with a falcon contumely to sweep
The site of all their dullard forms and flout
With sound of battle wave the battle dress.
Those functionaries of civic pride still smile.
The rest is clipping action down the walk,
Quick troops springing with clipped tread
Past files of grass and slipshod citizens.

As if a darkness spread to communicate
We veer as if we'd imitate
Those rebel and irregular birds
Though they are brigands, cannonading time.

For who who sees the birds rage off
Sees not his freedom and his choice prorogued?
For what is honor to the senator of goods?
All statues image our complacency,
All civic blessedness is scandalous.
Nor did we come to watch those soldiers prove
The discipline of learning death is just.

But some there are who bear more subtly than we know
A flagrant irresponsibility,
Aloft, proclaiming, to the skies.
Now let them pardon what we have to dread
And pardon that which acts upon us all
As if we had no guiltless chimeras
That haunt such public haunts as these.

Our anarchistic loves now bolt . . .
Their haughty innocence athwart
These dark ensigns they need not now condemn
Nor need atone for, freed from guilt.
It is the prime salvation of the sin, false flight!

O wondrous, black-necked water birds,
Drag the body, dazzle the heart,
And, under-lining of the black swan wing,
Submit us to this mire and fault.
O cycles of the rain and wondrous death
Of leaves that dye, enrich the lives
Of springs, repetitive summers, autumns, loss,
Dazzle the heart with woe and light
For what in us now constitutes the world
And world's revenge for the untimely fall
Of leaves that recapitulate our blight.

Apologia

AGOG, in rain house-deep,
Mud from the cars luxuriously
Splashed on feet, and lily leg
(In braces down from the knee),
The cripple lurched toward me.
She said: (O would you think
A beggar spoke so quick?)
Would you help me across the curb?
O she was pride-cheerful,
She cried: now don't you pity me.
Yes I will help you, I will
I will help you, I will, I will.

In quandry rain fell black
Muddy-eyed from the eye of night
And wind bent umbrellas back
(How many a skeleton lay on the walk!)
O you, I'd have said to her,
Disgust the callous deed I do.
Let watchers think I'm good, I'm not,
I'm caught in a deed I do not do
And false attendant thoughts about
The lots we're given, good or not,
And chance's power. or God's pity,
Banalities that black the heart!

I want to know, I'd have said,
What— is it faith?—makes you abide
This groveling step from side to side,
This stagger, wrench, galvanic bend.

Your effort's joke on all of us
Who walk from pride to shame in ease,
From fear to failure comfortably.

For the hurdle achieved, she smiled.
Her thanks like flowers bumped my nose.
O not the casual thought which ran
In anguish imitative after her,
Poor toady to infirmity!
Nor thoughts of justice, God's pity,
Nor that necessity to face
Reality with physical honesty,
Consoled the need I had to meet
Those penalties I was not guilty of,
That criticized the universe.

Addressed by her, it was to fear—
As at an accident's loud burst—
Some test of supplication there
Though why her passionate effort tasked
My abstract and appalling help
I could not understand.
I felt no love but dread.

O fear and pity sport
(Despair for the gay oppressed)
Like flies in summer light
(Is cruelest test)
Kill the sorry content, the guile,
The ethic splurge with which they go
Athwart the sun of honesty.

Deliver us to our despair
When looking glasses accost

The looking glass we are
And who mends which for who?
In ignorance infamous we beg
That veteran pain, and will.

False Country of the Zoo

WE ARE large with pity, slow and awkward,
In the false country of the zoo.
For the beasts our hearts turn over and sigh.
With the gazelle we long to look eye to eye.
Laughter at the stumbling, southern giraffes
Urges our anger, righteous despair.
As the hartebeest plunges, giddy, eccentric,
From out of the courtyard into his stall,
We long to seize his forehead's steep horns
Which are like the staves of a lyre.
Fleeter than greyhounds the hartebeest
Long-muzzled, small-footed and shy.
Another runner, the emu, is even better
At kicking. Oh, the coarse chicken feet
Of this bird reputed a fossil!
His body, deep as a table,
Droops gracelessly downwise,
His small head shakes like an old woman's eye.
The emu, ostrich, the cassowary,
Continue to go on living their lives
In conditions unnatural to them
And in relations most strange,
Remain the same.
As for the secretary bird,
Snake-killer, he suggests
A mischievous bird-maker.
Like a long-legged boy in short pants
He runs teetering, legs far apart,
On his toes, part gasping girl.
What thought him up, this creature

Eminently equipped by his nervous habits
To kill venomous snakes with his strong,
Horny feet, first jumping on them,
And then leaping away?
At the reptile and monkey houses
Crowds gather, to enjoy the ugly,
But mock the kangaroo who walks like a cripple.

In the false country of the zoo
Where Africa is well represented
By Australia,
The emu, the ostrich and the cassowary
Survive like kings, poor antiquated strays,
Deceased in all but vestiges
Who did not have to change, preserved
In their peculiarities by rifts,
From emigration barred.
Now melancholy, like old continents
Unmodified and discontinued, they
Survive by some discreet permission
Like older souls too painfully handicapped.
Running birds who cannot fly,
Whose virtue is their liability,
Whose stubborn, very resistance, is their sorrow.
See, as they run, how we laugh
At the primitive, relic procedure.

In the false country of the zoo
Grief is well represented there
From those continents of the odd
And outmoded, Africa and Australia.
Sensation is foremost at a zoo—
The sensation of gaping at the particular:
The striped and camouflaged,

The bear, wallowing in his anger,
The humid tiger wading in a pool.
As for those imports
From Java and India,
The pale, virginal peafowl,
The stork, cracking his bill against a wall,
The peacock, plumes up, though he walks as if weighted,
—All that unconscionable tapestry—
Till a wind blows the source of his pride
And it becomes his embarrassment—
The eye, plunged in sensation, closes.
Thought seizes the image. This shrieking
Jungle of spot, stripe, orange,
Blurs. The oil from the deer's eye
That streaks like a tear his cheek
Seems like a tear, is, is,
As our love and our pity are, are.

Elegy

Such folly to my heart renews
The silt of leaves and lisp,
I cannot hear that you are gone
As persons in their death must be
But hear you yet, in nothingness,
Renew your laughter till,
Irrational, all death of you
Is paradigm of irony.

Yet if absence is to lovers
Injury whose insolence
Studies in their wretchedness
Degrees of dying that they manifest
And absence is an ignorance
The simplest heart derives at last
A recourse from of subtle faith
(To find its consolations fast)
What of your death now grown so vast?

All departure is a threat
To sever rudely heart from root.
Who knows the journey knows what saves
When stations wait all durable in love.
Then old particular speech renews
Its strength in us like homeward earth
And certitudes are magistrate as rock.

But your departure posts no ways
Where deep are winter boughs with shade
The heart, deceived by happiness, did hang

Infatuate, a foliage on.
Nor huddled anywhere within a room
The past you left and could not give to me
That now transforms to death the deceived tree
And hurls illusory leaf on leaf down on
Your solitude that's brutalized by me.

For death is large whose entries are
Windy, white, and orotund.
There flesh increases every error it had.
Perhaps the soul, if it is free and is,
Examines there where nothing's real
The nature of reality.
No wonder that the sensual man turns back
To crack his laughter 'gainst the waiting urn.

Submission to that will I know
Not effects what changes I know
Not: (the worst of all). For to die
Is to be changed without knowing,
Is to be directed coldly, sport of prince
Whose genius digs in dingy dark.
As for you to die at all
Was for you to die more cruelly,
That is, to have me die in you.
Deserted I, I desert you.

(For summer hastes the worm
And nulls the sympathetic wound
And absolutes are relative
To death's dogged canopy.)

II

THE SUBJECT IS:

THE WORLD

V-J Day

FLAGS, effigies, the river broken out
With harbor whistles banging in the bay:
Wounds countermanded, guns shut up—
O is the national wound that coarsely camped
Promiscuously so wide and deep, now stopped?
The banks are purged and motorists may race.
Laughter, screams: on fire-escapes they kiss.
An anxious tax upon a bloody trade now spent.

This all keeps on, three days of it, as if
The dead were also dancing in their earth.
But what embattles these loud habitudes?
The heart's too coarsened and the mind too hurt.
This excess of the primitive is black.
Something unbearably painful drives the wind
Through streamers on the fire-escapes like flowers.
They rattle like old cerements or shrouds.

Eternal beasts make guiltless none of us
This thought resents us and disheartens tears.
We know no one exactly to address.
Sensations, brutalized, are more helpless
At hoping to invoke the name of Love.
The war was like a mouth who'd swallow us
And make us just exactly what it was.
Our armless men are all our statues now.

O what's the biggest stumbling bear
Goading invisibly, who will not dance?
The rocks have boiled and cities burst to stars.

Hot joy, some essence of your particle,
If such within the cold sky strive,
Convey against concussions of our thought
That we, that we may live, believe
We, serious in your uncaring, love.
And that may be the peace of some of us.

III

THE REAL ESTATE OF
THE HEART

From This There's No Returning

FROM this there's no returning, none,
Nor setting forth from out the centered night:
From this there's no appealing for release:
Captivity is torment that we want,
The only meaning that the wind has taught.

From this there's no returning, none
From this at night when in our arms we're caught
And irresponsibly time's worth we burn
And irretrievably are altered then:
From this there's no returning, none.

From this there's no returning though there is,
I do return, I must, though I would not.
What do I speak of then, what difference?
The touch that saw, love's better sight,
Is numb, for light is gone. And gone
The whole world of the body, gone.

The blood aches like the eye that cannot see,
The heart that heard its own at back of night
Now hears the roar of its disunity
And ever guilty of its want
The soul that heard its body lock it out.

O melancholy of analysis!
Break not your dark leaves here upon my thought.
The golden visage of the darkness came,
The wrath of morning was abated then
And, had I died in joy's perfection, I
Would I had died then.

What is this force that now sends out the day
To travel backwards to its source again?
What if I'm left and must endure alone
The cosmos that the agéd night upturned
When iron from its pole was outward drawn
And from the dark great images of sun?

Touch saw: or did you counterfeit the day?
Or you or night break through to bring what day
Or memory intensely hid? Or you
Or night that you, veined by great light so lay
Till memory its buried elations found
And memory like radium was freed?

Yet that which wrought a world so altering me
(What if I'm left alone and must endure)
Is like an unforgiveness here:
O origin I cannot cry for, praise,
That must so temper all my days
Teaches me too: we each must be alone.

O love, deceiver and deceived, remark
How close your torment that begins
Responsibilities you cannot hold for long!
For each of us must be alone.
It's circumstance the blood's brined in:
Wrong, wrong is done when we deny this to

Imitate perfection in a void,
Animal, forgetful, cry: we're world!
Wed disparities, defeats, to find
Two halves in one, two miseries allied
Till joy outrides its naturalness to be
Madness in union, death in unity.

O love, our demon sun, you cried to us:
You need not be alone for you may die:
Let us a madness, evil, so to think
We need not be alone until we die,
So stung and harrowed, heart-piercéd, we cry:
From this there's no returning till we die.

Labor and thought, O salvage us from this
Presumptive logic, dread paralysis!
That we, upon these plural routes traverse
'Twixt dual aptitudes the real, unreal
Nor robbing not a joy beyond its bounds,
Hold real, not unreal real, within our arms.

So negatives of these excesses nulled,
Nor joy affronting not reality,
We wrestle with profundities awhile
Where boisterous nature from its eminence
Looks on, approves, excels to reconcile
The dark and day that in espousals arm.

O intellectual dream that us exceeds
As nature's energy of forms defies
The imitative purpose of our pride!
We're pitched between these norms so to perfect
The heart that must endure its fear and hope,
The heart that must perfect its lonely want.

So to perfect and take a sweetness there
And bless the source of life that in us runs
Which seeks the purity it pours forth from:
O spirit air and winds invisibly that run
To marry in one direction sped,
And star that grazes on the mountainside

And earth to animals allied:
O blessed and blesser bound in us
That teaches how we must be unified
By what great purpose and whose holy pride.

Now Snow Descends

Now SNOW descends as if I'd gapped a grave
And all my heart is visible like death.
So you are gone who beggar all you gave
By still outvying what of you I have.
So you are gone and I am all your grave
Who long as longs the body for its soul
To turn the time which was its last, control,
Compose the sweetness that so ran,
And envy not the time that will not come,
Control, compose, and so then die again!

The snow now hastens to its formal rest.
So you are gone and I'm alone with ills.
Despair now seeks me as great longing starts.
Despair to know what I'm unworthy of,
Despair to know what changes as I breathe
So each farewell must seem its last and I
The laggard with what's both too quick and dear,
Left here with what now mutates in your sphere
Your lately joys become my harsh red north.

All this surrounds me like great stones,
Great stones the snow has covered delicately.
But if they move . . . I sit in darkness here
Until past pang, past common pang, and care,
I'm hunted to this last extremity:
To make one instant that you gave a life
Or by one word upon your cold soft mouth
Elucidate the action of your soul
By that one rose whose language is your myth.
(O snow that makes the wind too visible
And dares to tell enigmas of its wrath!)

Only the Irresistible Abides

AT THE crossing, wind-stricken in blow, I saw
Him of dead cares in penal fire.
The wind foully fell; the dung of the bird dropped.

Rough was the blast; rough clove bones to the beat
Flesh in such charge, shift.
Leaves drove backwards and forwards,
The horse reared; in the near distance sheep nudged,
Seeking determination of their warmth.

Crying aloud, my voice was snatched
Only to be tossed high like a leaf, empty
The word returned to my struck mouth.
Clearly going into my heart, had rolled back
His brow from its torment, his eyes from their penance.
What matter, cry of the wind hissing,
Sucking his face?
To my heart I trembled as radically changed the nature
        of him,
Spoliation, the bitter air of corruption.
Foresaw strength devoured by the weakness it came forth
        from,
The eye, flag of the war,
Dark light of the head, dark, hovered blood,
Cut tear, maniacal pity,
The smile bled by its subtleties there,
Killed pang, compassion, satirical mercy,
Sleep dead; the mouth closed like a grave upon
Traitorous censors, sweet frauds, hypocrites of the heart.

We passed: breath torn, bleeding,
I was at raw rock, dark the pit, roaring.
Foresaw his daemons with whom he contended,
Foresaw his battle running against him,
For the delicate conscience alone has embraced defeat,
Saw in spite of the issue always in question,
His lion-like labor.

Love, like those shadowy starlings wailing,
Plunged against buildings, their blind bodies falling,
Love, born to my breast, rose, more rugged
Than gust, blast, instructing his tyrants,
Infatuating his daemons, of his abyss defiant,
Courier caught sweet blood of his tears, sweet anguish
   wrung,
Though roaring the tongues of the wind as his name
I came to through valleys of evil, of honor
Resisting no evil nor knowledge that the soul endeavor
World in him.

Conjectural Domain

IF HE is he without the royal perception
Is like that question asked by those who gain
Sight that will identify nothing:

And do I clothe him with the eye of lilies
And dress him with the wilderness of nations,
His subtle heart the sea flora

I wreak from voyages through those wiles
The imagination sickly conquers?

Then what herbs control his will
And grassy sleep is his where he is not?
For I'd impel him most impossibly to be

All that he is each instant,
His Protean selves in nuances so jeweled
And Himalayan opposites so met—

Perfection of knowability!—till he is whole
Like angels who shine forth, no dark stain visible.

Desire walketh in darkness like the fool.

For I who study him may know
No more of me than what I must infer
From hooded rat who eats his own father

Or centaur whom I may not know at all.

But as the deer seeks rarest herbs
To expel the wound from his hunted breast,
I seek, oh difficult cure, thy flower, commending

His mystery to all its eminence
Which to accept is the most anguished task,

Whose glitter, turning within the vast unknowable,
Perception grasps and can't let go,
Cold Adam of improbables,

Sweet centaur of the philosophical manuals!

Homage to Ghosts

ALWAYS within me lies
That former form of experience
If suddenly I bare my eyes.
Always dismembering me, although
It is so altered and so changed
I know it and know it not.
O, I ponder that time set
Some things beneath its yoke
And set not it
And yet my passion and my want
Built a lasting place wherein
Obediently it lies
And still evades all consequence
Of an ordinary demise.

But I see that even mind
Alters substance between time.
In those years it has lain there
I grew different, and my change,
All unknowing, made it strange.
The image that it lay in me
Was subject as I was to all
Shocks that made my soul grow ill,
Took account of every sorrow,
And of my body did so borrow
Till I think that what was it
Is now, surely, only me.

Still, it has such separate power
It forbids all I would touch

And takes away the life from what
Is living, though it is not.
Perhaps it is my tomb as well,
For both of us without conjunction
Lie prison stones on recollection.
But thought, despite such memory,
Yet tears the soul from the body.
I love and do not love
And indifference and fidelity
Between their greeds fast with me,
My bones plucked dry to satisfy
That double eternity.

Song

MY LOVE commits me to his care
I want not when my love is near
He is the rose on which I fare

O tree bend down your boughs my dear
That of your joy my joy I dare
Taste like your leaves and fruit, my dear

For he commits me to his care
Rose, envy not, nor moon in your cold lair
Felicity I do not fear

For he is merciful as air
And he commits me to his care
I cannot die when he is near

Song

O BEAUTIFUL, my relic bone,
Whitening like the foreign moon,
Whose lustre consummates my tomb.

O beautiful, my flesh rose-grown,
Rose-rose white from that small bone
Whose vapor is the breath I own

And tendrils of my blood curl in.
Rose-rose white, the flesh I am
But murderer eye and murdered!

For all the flesh becomes an eye:
I am no flesh while yet eye's eaten
The rose-rose flesh bare to the bone,

Bare to the bone! But that flesh still
By heat of dew renews again.

O bless, occurrence of the moon
When actual flesh of both is gone,
My flesh the air the eye takes in,

That flesh on bone the air the eye takes in,
Death-wedding the moon shines in.

The Double Praise that Simplifies
the Heart

YES! I would keep you from all who love you!
Call me jealous, decline my fanatic will!
What's love that is not arrogant 'gainst those fools?
They can't fly straight from their desire to you
But, shameless with fear and greed, connive
Traps for your volatile essence that runs like water
Past all mooring and straight from owning.

In the uxorious summer disordered by August
I think, to endure sensation's fire,
Of white wind and the abstract shade.
This day is the coxcomb of the year!
Like an invalid returning to health I lie
Naked to light which the wind bends toward me.
Sufficient the senses to the green of the eye!

But the reflective emptiness of fields
Whose vacancy was philosophic like the sky
Is taken over by the coarse, woody life of the weeds
And the clatter of insects littering the view.
And I fear for the summer burning away
As I fear for the vigor consuming your soul
(The restless leaves against the mountain turn).

Though now is the day to pluck raspberries, hot, dear
And ripe, they plague the bedeviled thirst of the tongue.
The air eats my body, your heart eats my heart
And the shade of the mountain must wither and fall.

O you are unknown here and for you I thirst.
I am drunken and blind on the earth's fleshliness.
(The cloudy hollows in the mountains start.)

What if they love you too and must own you
As I must own the day that torments me?
They love you as poor humans who must die
And I love you as mountains vie with clouds,
Are towered by them and wreathed by their small dew
(For clouds must indicate the mountain's soul
And prove the lurk of further joy.)

And I love you as one whose sight is poor
So judge you flawless (as I vow) you are.
What visions labor them but desperateness?
Are they haunted by sight to hunt your soul
Or, arms cast round you, mocked by what
Drives out the instant from the common lot
To parody the blood with spectral thought?

Yes! I would keep you from all who love you!
Claiming you as I claim the mountains and fields.
O, you take up image and space as the mountain
Takes up the earth and that makes me proudly,
Perceiving the flood and rough storm, marvel
At those who love only in part and shrewdly.
(The fury of nature teaches me honesty.)

For I see we are as wild in the crucial blood,
If such madness surrounds us we too must be mad
And the stones cast up by the earth and angry water
Mock us who beg: are we symbols or they?
And the woody mountains disdain reply

And the green material of distance drilled
By the rabbit and badger and butterfly.

Now tempt and connive with those others.
That is your will. I can do no more
Than praise and perceive you in the pierglass of time
And your soul that permits to my solitude
The burning negation of death and pride
And permits me equality to fly naked and mad
Into the substance of fear and perfection.

Yes! I would keep you from all who love you.
No one else was so born to praise you.
You endow no one else with the knowledge and fire.
Then rightfully I keep you from all who love you.
Arrogance is the humility and mystery
That let you permit me in time
Find the fire that will burn me through.

Old Haven

DIRECTIONS that you took
Which told me how I could
Amid those cultured streets describe
My rude impulse to you,
Now turn within my head,
Signs tangled while I sought
Good milkmen who could set me straight.

As those on bicycles
Who asked me was I lost
And mouldy houses that concurred
With cornices to bless,
All proved such lesson of
Love's reassuring depths.

The churches of the place
And dear, pastured squares
Like museum objects borrowed
An ancient air to please
Till dim old gentlemen
Like robin goodmen winked
And sprightly dogs were unicorns.

Now absent from you, dear,
My fatuous joy declares
How love may change a city, give
Glee to horses pulling
Loads, to gutters virtue
And to salesmen, grace.

For smile so sweetly those
Tottering cupolas, old
Curbs in my enamoured thought (where
Spongy Florida steals
The stale New England air),
I ponder on love's strength,

So cunning when direct,
So roguish when sincere!
If dogs may charm because you're there,
Drugstores infatuate,
And meanest citizens
Like saints from niches step
To guide me to your goodness and to luck.

Solitary Discourse Broken in Two

AND STILL you burn the cigarette
And sit on my French chair
And laugh as little children used to do.

So occupy your absence with your glance
As if the room held you
More truly now than when you're here. Untrue!

When actually you're here once more
My thoughts of what I take you for
And all the way the light takes you

Cannot tell if they're more real
Or that self you know as true.
Your nearness breaks both worlds in two,

The entity I suffer, for I would
Hope to love just what?
Desire so wants you kind to me!

O, O, but intermittent gravities
Weight silence with profundities
And the long look in your eyes

Begins again my pieties—
To distort or understand?
I do not know. O, O, to lie

With you like children under leaves!

For just as now, it seems,
To look at one another, we
Set part a time and hide the way

Our eyes then stray,
As if we found and ate
This sweetness which we generate.

Which, is it true? Which, would you do?
Desire so clouds my sight
In willful ignorances throughout!

The Mask and Knife

AND I would have you clad like dominoes
In every stripe and lozenge you would dare,
A gauged discord, irregular and clair,
Or corsleted in ribands like a beau.

Be armed by shells, those profits of the Sound,
As, slippered like a prince in modesty,
You softly fly the docks as coarse sail cloth
Swelled by the wind and sailing bluely north.

I'd have you move as springs unwind the Flood
Or as a perfume galls the scrupled blood,
I'd have you yoke me till I could not break
Though broken I as uncouth horsemen might

Bully a spirit to its brink.
O jacketed like dandies in a silk!
I'd have you rayed and tangled in douce ropes
As on triumphal sea-mouths of the north

The hawser founds its ship at captive ports
Odor of fur, a belle cool din!
Till then the shock of some dark pose
Falls like a music deepening seas

Or like your name whose lips make weights in me.
Abyss, who harbors my infirmities,
The angels of your eyes are all my foes.
Now forward gaze nor deepward gaze no more

But backward gaze to gaze me into hell.

Primer of Plato

ALL ENDEAVOR to be beautiful:
The loved and the loveless as well:
All women rob from duty's time
To pitch adornment to its prime.
The lion in his golden coat
Begets his joy by that; his mate
Beneath that fiery mane repeats
The fury of each sudden sense.
The swan reflecting on the stream
The opposite feathers of the swan-
Webbed dream is like the fox at night
Who glows as in original delight.
Not least, the sun in tedious round
Bestows on rock and land
Principles that all creation
Imitates in adoration.

I never knew this till I
Chanced to see how your bright cheek
Brightened from the gaze of one
Who swam a spirit's Hellespont.
I saw then that beauty was
Both for lover and beloved a feast,
The lover mirroring by his joy
That flush beauty brings, in
His eye her actual face globed small,
And beauty flattered by that glass
Pitched to its highest comeliness,
Doubled and increased until
All would seem

Derived back into first essence.
Both animals and men dwell
In such a mirror of the real
Until in sudden ecstasy
They break the boundaries of that glass
To be the image each first was.

"Marriage Is a Mystery of Joy"

OLD IMAGES beset the scoundrel eye:
Adornment for the ceremonial bride
Whose joy was consecrated by the torch:
Behold the serpent married in that wine
When, green as Eve, she pledged a worldless world
To time's iron strictures and oblivious lust.

That banquet glows upon the startled eye:
It'd seem the image is enough, enough
Its seizure cold and rude as death.
But imagery's a desert of desire
And kills the sense as quickly as it maims
The heart on which it feeds but which it starves.

And sight's immediacy needs more of proof.
The soul's soon worn: the body grows jealous:
Some further wedding in the fleshless shade,
Needs be set forth that apes no mummery
But sets to music what the eye brings forth
And kiss substantiates the praiseful tongue.

What absence, soul of winter, and the first
Of deaths, could consecrate negation of,
Let presence then absolve before the dawn
And like an island set with her small face
Famish the world until the year be gone
Though ruddy fools by their desire be slain.

Then fish be caught for her and young swans baked
As tribute lavished by her rival's realm

ERRATUM

By an unfortunate error four lines and three stanzas were omitted when "Marriage Is a Mystery of Joy" was printed. They should have been placed at the top of page 55.

Music attend her sentried motion till
The gliding foot is gloved to air's concert
And marriage of ascent and impulse that
Halts the war of matter for a while.

Here's cockatrice! Here's hawk and espial dress!
The measured entries to the wake of kings!
Heaped high the rosy fruits and dandled flesh
Spoil of the seasons and the world's concern!
While skewbald cranes, like leprous sovereigns, pick
Desolate ways amid that joy's precincts.

Still is the moment bantered by its haste!
On that exchange where dual souls then pledge
War upon their infidelity's waste
Soon image crowds between the air and head.
Now ponder on imponderables and beat
The flesh attenuated to fine shade!

For she's already lost in abstraction:
The sea's empire that banquets her has gone
With Venus whose old trophies load the blood.
The wedding's wake, for she's eclipsed by that
Belaboring of perfection brandished like
The lightning's fuse that scarifies the stone.

'Who's deserted by existence then?' We,
Who saw her once and never can know peace
And go, rejecting *longeurs* of eternity,
In love with sense, crying for wilderness
Of that, proportion like the joke of spring
Till she is queen of heaven, vision seen

From which we wander till we die, never
Absolved in search nor granted solace twice.
Sight breeds dream on dream and that's our doom!
We're poised and caught 'twixt what we can't possess
But what we'd will the world away for now.
Like acrobats in trapeze instant, we

Going and coming between paradox,
Must live upon that world's point, peak
Where ideality has hid her like a snow.
Obsession with the real imprisoned us.
Experience set expression at a loss
And desolate Edens mocked us everywhere.
Self knowledge was a rankling substance then.

Now: we exist to be her glassy sea,
Not only imagery, but medium
Which she might drown in as we're drowned, quite lost,
But happy to be lost, for we are found
In courts of princes and of infidels
Imagination's, that is, liar's realm.
This is the only solution love may find.

IV

THE METROPOLITAN

TRIAL

Oration Against the Orator's Oration

FROM the mouth of that fanatical fire
Grew private senses fantastical,
Chalk shadows on the leaf-cold lawn.

He stood before the frost-stropped roofs
Where blackened leaves flopped round his head
Like crows no longer squawking in a wood.
He stood in the mobbed center, their haranguer,
Fop prophet, fop angel, their transformer,
This wing-haired being, wooing their old sores.
Their smile upon his words lit up his head.
The woody plane that drummed here now and then,
The slack pilasters and distempered courts,
The ramps and trucks, hot congress of
The deuced dilemma, vermin, itch—
All that surrounds them as they are, is gone!
Some words are pistols that explode the head,
New shores unflag, build new and unplagued houses.
The world is being made again for them.

But the function of the intellect is to move,
Move, move, against the blazing night,
Though the office of the sail be tired and dirty,
The water pocked and rabid, on the shore
The effecting of a promise that outbids
The actual coming of a gift or peace
Much as the hope outweighs the imported letter.

Move, move, I cried, his oratory is stale
And birds other than the starlings soar

Abused, abusing, to the cloud.
Let them stream up and scatter all the cloud.
You make them names, you cry batallions of names,
You set the cosmos in your own order
And clap them in that cosmos round your heads.

But there they stand like showcase smiles.
Rank and inert, they're not to be unmoored.
They stand as if he were Pythagoras
Who shines the window-glass of their thick world.
To those who think they comprehend by love
In all places he is seen at once, he is
Their green and carnal ignorance.

But, as wind swirling, moves shadow and birds,
Blowing the course of the bullet north degrees,
Planting its form on the thick tree
And becomes the tree, blowing a surf of leaves,
You birds come here, you birds dive, dive,
Now let one person, I myself, dare move.
O there is a swirl of thoughts the wind
Makes singular, there are the senses that extend
Until the blank eye is a life of green,
Gradations of a shade, there is the earth.

What living thing does not outgrace
A battering ram, a gross artillery
A *p* over *t*, a junket of word-mouthed words?
I see the world, it's propped by argument,
Vast pillars set to support a windy pride,
Pediments acanthus-bound, entablatures,
All ways to keep the ego up and sun
As if we couldn't bear the world
Unpropped, unbooked, and unreasoned.

O the appalling wreck, the disfigured world,
The moon all sliced, disheveled, disembowled!
The fresh winds blowing whose vocal
Not now one instant curbs our grimy nouns
Nor lets us hear one instant silences
As if the senses could not bear the world
All naked, maculate and faulty,
And five green senses then but all the Word.

"Enemy of the Body"

SUMMER agog now on alley and street
Dense on the sidewalk, sexy and public,
Old roach of the seasons, is drunk on its swill,
Smell, infection, convulsion of engines,
The stench of doorways and odium of stairs.
All released, voices pent by the winter
Concite and promote the commotion of
Babel: all's a-swarm in the soured air
With racket and flies, fire escapes gorged
With animals, cries, in the termagent sun.

Yet orchards unburdened prove now their weight
With dusky their windfall, the connubial plum.
The shade now is clustered. cloudy and deep.
O explorers, thigh-foundered, your heads turned by Eden!
While deuced and unfanned, the grimy bathers
Gather in congress at the used sea
Whose cantankerous waters are sooty and tackled
By saturnine cruisers smoking offshore.

Dead-Life Study

Look down the airshaft where the windows stare:
Old kitchen rags and peel line this steep well,
Our mouldy closure where the roaches swag,
Intoxicated on communal swill.

Here sounds rampage; wind squeaks or child-like screams
In this collective null and rats forage,
An old man hacks, a prisoned terrier yawps
Where, 'mong these discards, we have foisted hell.

Disheveled patients on your stony beds
Like hedged-in infants wailing in a ward,
Is this the propagation of our dead?
Is this the ending to eternity?

"There Is No Anti-Semitism in the Village".. POLICEMAN

SCUFFLE and hue of cries, a sudden blow:
Running and hastily running: language of
Sores. Volley, not rumor now. A bottle falls.
What's lying in the street face down?
Brave boys, gorgeously ganged, gang round.
They kick him in the head, jammed there.
They are kicking a man in the head to death.
What intercession from the slept-in hair
Of sluggish waked-ups staring down?
Their heads hang out as at a fire, one cheers
And someone comes. A car As fast they can
As roaches run, those boys scatter. Some blood
Is lying in the street likewise.

The goggled shades sit back into themselves.
Cold thickens like a grease upon the night.
He wrenches, falls, gets up again, he goes.
Vomit of silence succeeds. We are done.
Night like a greasy scum now thickens round.
Undone. Fragmented like glass our gay union.

Poem

I SAW the mountains in a rose-fire light
Upon my ill-housed street, whose old-law flats
Were stained a blood light, rose-christ light,
How fiery sweet!

Those mountains of the sun I saw,
All peaked and small, like waves that stabilize
Their pearl, or crystallize into a snow
Their light, all cast aboundingly from out
The fiery brim, the golden den of night.

As if a skiey flame could crucify
Our lives, the prisons of conceptual plight,
I saw, I wept, for we were all burning,
Our faces all, in crucibles of light.

Immutable vision of the beautiful
That changes once and once again with light!
A cloud cast on the sun its ire.
That flaming and descending sun did then depart
And it was grey, the first of night.

I saw how easily we start—
Our hearts in us that so desire the fire.
I saw and wept and we were all.
I saw and wept, my cheek did burn.

Vision and illusion, oh return!
That I with joy and fire and light
In fire and light and delicate joy my life
May live in crucibles like that, and burn.

The Drunk

GONE to the state of childishness or evil
The drunk feels free now to do everything,
Give him a tree and he will be an ape,
A gun and he will murder like an infantry
Or dance or fornicate or puke or sing.
He is a most bold and a most free man.
Carnivorous of philosophy, he spews
All grudges, secrets out, a macaw fuss.
Is this the dignity of India, is
Honor like a fat one's belly loosed,
Has reticence no further pangs than this?
The drunk is no one, he is gone awhile,
Crowding upon his knees and bawling "Mother!"
Or else in doorways sprawls with scarlet head
Freed of his name, responsibility,
Known to only blood and libido.
He is instinctual endlessness—the eternal state
Of always being never individual,
And sleep is like foul earth upon his chest.

Banquet of the Utilitarian

THE DEBRIS of use chokes us immoderately:
Tin cans and clinkers, crates and peelings sit
On sidewalks, moderators of our contumely.
Eggs sucked and chairs dismembered, rubber tires,
The quarrel of nail with wood, old shoes and ash,
Now pile supreme to us their rabid heaps,
Mountain on mountain in a rash of power.
When will their junk, exceeding all our needs,
Outdo th' ambitious agent starting this?

But what as victors of environment we
Can do, we'll leave to dumps and dirty seas,
Which less pollute the lily's stenching foot,
Till all we did disorders what we do,
Impediment more herded than those yards
Where, huddled in disuse, protruberant,
Sits scrap that will not budge, which disaffects
Unlike the dead, each local year its sweets.

LETTER

Letter for Vadya

To SOME, guests come like a career,
With volley of love, excessive charm, and news,
And so they come to you at any time
In drear, mad rain, or afternoon,
Gay from the train or long boat ride.
If so at any time they come, the door
Always open and the hour always ripe
For talk and wine, the rage of politics
And brief excursions to the ethic side
Of the aesthetic, or the pure kinetic,
That's hospitality, they'd say.
What's hospitality? I'd say. I'd rather say
Some sense impression ineffaceable:
The single rose so gathered to itself,
Crossing the air with its most subtle guile,
The foreign books, portfolios of painters,
And our dear Chekhov in his chequered pants
Who smiles from out the youthful album of the past.

If so guests come, I came, to plead
A banal migraine of the soul
And sudden loneliness that shook the heart
As wind will shake an old, decaying house.
(But who is sad in summer colonies
And who's subjective at the beach or *spa?*)

Huddled with gloom against the public bar,
I'd spent one-half the afternoon
Like any bum who hopes to drink
His childhood conscience down the drain;

And drinking, heard resentfully old jokes
On mother-in-law with temperance hatchet armed,
The comic necessity for sex, et cetera,
The crazy wisecrack and the vaudeville gibe;
Ignored, envied, repudiated then
That chumminess those compromisers bragged
Who, merely afraid, refused to let
Their past declare a war on them:
Those loud-faced farmers, card-game touts, one pale,
Promiscuous girl, drunks talking of dead wives:
Who, merely afraid of incidents
No sooner born than buried, ganged up against
That knowledge of their differences,
So drowned in laughter's dreadful unity
The alien cry from corners of the soul
Of lost, aware, and lonely consciousness—
So proved, it seemed, how 'collective man' betrays
Essential state, O private-public guilt,
Which it is never best to think of or admit!

That riff-raff of loose talk exiled me to
Some disconnection with the real.
At least a wildness pounded in my head,
Some old rebellion fitted out to be
The frightened carriage of the self past fear.

Where was the trusted and familiar then?
I sat in panic like someone who wakes
To find himself in a strange room
Faced by his friends who've all grown alien masks,
Eyes bulging, with distorted mouths,
A cold and unforgiving hate deranging
All reasonable and loving orderliness.
And thought, then, of the night-long walk—

Some anodyne to null my great malaise—
The bus-ride to the last blue mountain line—
And thought of sleeping in a field somewhere
Divided by small rivers, wheat and woods.
Of course I could go home and kick the doors,
Read furiously, or weep the critical tears.
The human heart's a joke, I thought.
Such platitudes then sought their favorite cage
As *free* or *acted on.* I asked
"My animal trainer then?" but spurned the rage. . . .

O what decision deep, irrational,
Will lead us to those boldnesses of deed
Whereby the faith's expended on a word
The hope's contracted from a vision of
Some soaring of the sweet contrition of the Dove?
But rhetoric's to no avail!
Suffice it that I thought, Vadya, of you,
No sooner thought than wished to see you then
And found a nickel burning up my hand.
So planets of our desolation move
Our choice propulsions with a grand flourish
And we, defiant of those spies, rejoice.

When I arrived the night was tough,
And lightning wracked and jarred the nervous clouds.
Your guests were all set up for cards,
Stakes for deuces wild, the knave of hearts.
And will you join, they asked, while I declined,
Choosing to take my chance with rum and port
And kitchen privileges of less public talk.
(Need I forget how Mishka welcomed me
As if I were his long-gone equal soul
Returned from some lost Paradise of Smell)

And so we talked beneath the kitchen bulb.
The game of chance was running fast while we
Discussed the artist's anonymity,
And his 'most sinister conditions' of creativity.
Some other subjects too, all grave attempts
As if the *real* must then be exorcised
Or all its demons would eat up the heart. . . .

So talk went on and suddenly it was late
And I was tired, too tired to go away
And so stayed on, the unexpected guest,
As if I were the skeleton at the feast!
So stayed upon the corner sofa in
Sleep half-waking as one sleeps with fever,
So sleeping waked the dancers thronged around
The ghost of rose, some existential scent
Surpassing earthly flowers, so sleeping, woke
And slept, alternately hot with great forgiveness,
Cold with solace, terrors gone but some small shame
That I had had to plead for what's most natural,
The private sorrow of the unreachable soul,
Dragging at my heart like a dark wind.

And suddenly the cats came in! That great dog
Tried to kiss me, birds began
Within the green shell of the light
Their small dispersals 'gainst the rational dawn.
The sun burst out! The child came down,
Aloof and bold and cleanly from her sleep,
Pleased to find so much altered,
I the unknown, stowaway in a corner,
And guests within the ante-rooms.
And vines and porous cheeks of leaves all crossed,
Ingrained and interleaved by fallen rays,

Made all the windows matchless mouths of caves
As if their squares were fibers of the sun,
A virile hardiness that cut across
And ached and burned the eye with its pure self:
Pristine assembly of the senses all,
Tincture of the angelic universe,
Pure morning poised upon the year's climax.

So soon the house was up, breakfast was on,
With all its appalling need for social appetite,
And soon like tourists on a holiday,
We all set off to hike the long way round
Past cliffs and verges and cold falling brooks,
A tropic way to marketing for you
A foreign way for me to home again.

And dreamy then with certitudes
Half-changed by images that had no place
In intellection or sobriety, I thought:
We have a right to pleasure when
It's strong and certain as the sensational sun!

So here's some small account of an event
Whereby you let me, Vadya, be my worst:
Most stupid, miserable, and honest.
Perhaps I thank you that you let me come
Bringing my griefs as guests would bring you grapes,
Or nectarines and melons heapéd high.

But now the account's at end, what moral comes?
Green was the wind and world and green my heart.
I speak of simple, incommodious things like joy.

At least, in a world of cold acceptances
I dream a sanguine innocence may come
As comes the rain or from the mountains, doves,
And every generous action move again
The springs of some gay spontaneity.

Our joys are nameless, like our truest will.
To speak in symbols is an enterprise
The rose has learned whose impetus is free.
Dear friend, I write to learn what symbols may,
In visions of that tender climate, breathe,
Where thought is but some local symmetry
Sensitive as the rose, to warmth and light,
And all our talk a way of being that.

VI

SOUL'S ZOO

Enemy of Those Who Are Enemies
of Sleep

O MOON my mask,
Clear in the nightwoods now you lie,
Tilted upon your halved and garroted face.

O moon my mask,
Dealer of actions lewd and forced,
Upon the unlettered waste,

O moon, sweet task, white face,
O white, O sweet, my oval glance,
I turn, I turn, from your empowering glass.

O now . . . for whose engrossing force . . .
Although by pitchpine you are borne
Or tusked by mountains you are flung,

Your leafage, play, your stamps of intricacy,
O moon, intemperate tenement. convict
Like a clown's great gloves, the trademark

For, or hairy maps and biscuits of
Day's convert dragging us through pits.
O moon, sweet angelology of fall,

Your parts and terminals of light,
Before you're out, must win, despite . . .
For in our sleep you breed our dreams for us

Half children of your sensual tyranny,
By whose Urania gods and cats
In equal heat, conciliate your snows

And we, by your sphered music, top
White forms, fair senses, eastern genii that
Launch summers just as soundlessly

As all the engines of eternity.
O nuptial drug and condiment of rite,
O tempter to an inwardness of sight,

Dwarfs, indigo, within whose opera,
O bridal jest, you circummortal us,
Nuptial of vacancy who wizards us.

And all the fur of suns is not worth you
Burning in empty hamlets our abstracts
Whose shadows close behind us like a door.

In Praise of That Epic, Dream

WRACKED by the seas sprung of the Venus,
By the green loin hairy and the rough sand tongued,
Clad by scales of the bosom early
Neither mermaid nor child nor the goddess fully,
Spun by the pearls of the girt shells rounded
Bounded like breasts, those medallions of honor,
From elements gasping where the sun greenly
Cast down its ball like an octopus eye:

I was this, neither living nor being:
Duplicate of the desire in my resting:
By windows invaded and the next doorway,
Bare-breasted my wishes swam to me;
I was this as the ship folded downwards
And the eyes of all creatures fastened on me
And I on their own selves my destiny settled,
Venus arranger, arrigner, O spinner.

Stars like a ganglion of my own centre
Collapsed and collided in my down speeding,
Venus now mast-tall, roofed me with foam,
I cleft the great spiral as the hour brimmed.
I was this then, lapped in the morning
Till that magnet and spindle of North,
Antipodes to my knowledge and force,
Dived under my hand, in the middle of minute

Shot through the cold of my angry arm,
Swam through the vein, through protest and pride
Mixed with the lymph and milk of my mother,

From the blond cocksureness of blue-veined father
In confidence struck, then smiled at the clanging;
The valves like a mollusc shuttered in fright,
Aorta resounded the land of my hate,
Sea water flooded my nervous heart out.

This was the pearl found, the Venus breasted,
This was the twin of the sea and the morning
Knocking announcement as it came through the window,
My body prone lifted, my sleep carried away;
Servant of it, the master no wiser,
I sank by those threads that pulled the ship down,
Arion denouncing, said the low song
Sea death and land lock, no captor to save,

As Venus the mother in her soft realm
Shrank in her bubble to monster stillness,
Shrank like a spider though extending her power
Everywhere radiant from her dark center,
Out of itself its tissues delighting
Strand-thin as the milk from the breasts of her foam,
Lightness and bubble become my great home
And killer like sailor, the mighty, my martyr.

Iowa City Zoo

THAT ring-necked pheasant, feather-worn,
Drinks water grey-scummed, his snake eye
Sullen in no gratitude, leaves thick on wire
Of chicken cage; the sun falls in
Through escaped feathers and the taint of leaves.
It's arbitrary, that roof the Autumn's blown.

Delicately the rabbit drinking catches
His chin hairs there; they're limp from weight.
A black wife hunches in the farther dark.
The turkey hens are crying frugally,
Their heads in a maze of discontent.
Shoo their turkey-cocks toward them!

Look: their dirty runways, races, water,
Their leaky houses, battered turnips, grain
Rotting (mauve doves peck at the soiling floor,
Their eyes diamonded by curious zest—the blood
That shines there through the eye?) What dignity
Affronts offal! Security that cannot be disarmed!

But wall-eyed deer, the lilacs fed you well.
Since you are blind, your eyes are all of us.
When will we trip and fall upon their look,
That bugled eye, that marble-sick uniqueness?
The rabbit's shamed who drinks dewfall
And you in your detention here
Have dulled our natures with your spartan glitter,
As misery embarrasses the poor.

Movie Montage

(For Col. Dick Johnston)

SLEEP, padded like a vacuum where we sink—
The movie, trusty robber of our consciousness
As with horse, dog, the elastic riders,
We go west to home, we go west to ramshackle
Old ranges, we go west to old mortality
Where grandma in her bonnet calls the changes
Sleep, suction, and the limitless derangers—
Let us go west where ports are new like barges
And moose, taller than towns, stalk in the bay.
O whiskey bar, broad as leviathan
Where men submit their restlessness to cups
And swill the fiery stuff like solvent water.
Let us go west where home is with the horses
And clap the bar with hand as broad as boards.
What if the town is painted on like eyebrows,
A wind could blow the clapboards off,
The grey, dejected, slapdash buildings fold
Like jackknife bridges and all be lumber
Where nails of wormy boards stand up askew
To bruise the nose of unsuspecting dogs?
Still, talk of childhood's here, where errors began:
As well: attractive freedom, riding into town
After a long winter among the cows.
Then peril lurks, convenient as the hills
From whence help cometh if you ride to them:
The old big-gut who slouches on the porch
Eager as nemesis to track you down,
The old judge, dressed like cavalry, made fat
On flies he's swallowed in his sleep:
Well, these are figures in the human plot

And tell the sum of action like a book.
If action is the man, the man's declared
Like trophies to the customs judge.
The trifle, that is, that has crooked his heart,
The trifle, perhaps, that would set him straight.

This is the movie where we stalk the past
As husky bailiffs trek the rustler down.
O double-action cast in shadows there!
So freed by actions immigrant to us
(The cowboy's romance with his horse)
We set ourselves before this silver screen
To track oblivions to their lair.
To set the body down in images:
That is what we strive, we struggle for,
To render from an ideality
The lust of senators and buffaloes
While cattle bellow out who're pent in night
And faithful, sick-eyed dogs wait in the cold
Visibly thin, and shivering off more weight.

VII

BROKEN-NOSED GODS

I

IF LOVE possessed us once
What treason now employs our hearts in hate?
It is a felony
That both our hearts are critic dry with wit
And tongues but good for talk.

Has age, your busyness, or time
Or repetition, brought us this?
Or are we wearied, and crave
Stronger effects to wake
The old mortality so ill in us?

Come! Aren't we wearied? To be
More glad to go than stay,
Bitter-adept as now we are
At scorn—insult, not praise,
Rebuke with roughcast injury,
No tenderness but scalding lies?

But once habitually we met
Intent, invested in a dream,
As if, two natural objects, we had been
Enjoined to join.
Acted we not volitionally?
Sleep partakes of such a property—
So fine is all the will,
So fiery fine the senses then,
All but a literal paradise disowned.

89

But that was then, and now—
Propulsion that is not
Exultance of a rage
Drives us forth and back.
With coldest eyes we dare
The wound to kill, the ultimate death of those
Old selves that made big vows.
We scrape the moonlight off the house,
We throw our rings at walled lilies
Enseamed around the room's once old, old rose.

Our factoried hearts incendiary—
So hot a thing is hate—
Begin ancestor-worship, praise
The lowly infinite!
If emeralds come from Colombia,
If rocks can change the discourse of a sea,
Have we degraded, disvalued
Love's necessary enmity
Or, exhausted true concourse,
Found import but a nullity?
Is it the realization of experience?
Is it the years' morality?

Love may breed from hate again
Or hate breed love anew
But there's a hatred that is whole
Which may not turn from its own soul
But, Narcissus-fascinate,
Repudiates the all.
Is this our ill?

II

To go into the morning like a thief
To ascertain one's spirit grief
And thence to kill one's love outright
That had bounded day and night
My soul prepare! whose anguish knows
To what exiling dark it goes.

To kill one's love that one may be
Mutinous in liberty
And walk forthright in coldest sorrow
Because one could not love the more
When faults and petty crimes haste all
Consumption of the false Idea!
And one must hate what injures now—
The past proved all deceptive—though
More bitter is the future that is null.
As for the present, it is powerful
With images begot of death and hell.

To go into the morning like a thief
Since one has now no right by any faith
To dare a robust, unflawed strength
For one, thenceforth, is but the heir of night
And fens and paths forbidden to the light.
To rob, kill, cast out primal joy
Because one must, through what necessity,
Abjure what cannot help one now.

III

If love must lose its action and its strength,
Then hail to ours, its mingy, dull decline!
Belabor me for making out last year
An icon false as any one-legged throne
And honor me who now have seen your eyes
For what they're worth and what they're not in me.

If love must lose its action and its strength
Is this then hate, this dearth of excited thought?
Or death of the hope to see perfection grow
By bearing image 'gainst the false-sweet soul?
What have I to learn if it's not this
Or be if I cannot escape this heart of error?

What of the image that I tear at now?
Clown of the reason, mimic of the will!
I loved my images far more than you
As partial as the seasons aren't, or death,
Who gave perfection you aspired not to,
And vowed you were what you'd not be at all.

Thus so disdaining prime reality,
Sufficient is the irony for me.
For comes the essential, startling spring.
I'm covered to its brutal green,
Am like the dead who nourish not one dream,
Am mythless as a scientist or beast.

And go to smell the moon and joke the trees,
Dispassionate and changeless like those rocks
Who're gashed from the old stone of earth,
Or squat and saurian inmates of such Farms
As where the poor go when they're almost gone
Prolonging painful lives for hateful guards.

IV

How weary, cold, unreal, the heats of love,
Exuberance of the ego, fictive lie!
Now that the self has spent the burning coin
How counterfeit its value and its shine
As if the feel of metal in the nervous hand
Transferred itself unto the kissed-out mouth,
The taste of metal sour and acid on
The rosy mouth that drank the apple in.

How weary, cold, unreal, the heats of love
When witnessed from the center of the eye
That is, itself, the center of dead lust
And is, itself, the apathy of death.
Now go, old love, now go and be you dead
Fictive illusion, motive of the ego!
That labors like a charlatan to dress
Scarecrows of form and bandy-legged youth.

Now go: self sees the carrion-lie it has invented
Out of the frenzy to be frenzied by activity.
Rest is the natural center of the soul
Where solitude and dread impersonality
Receive, accept, judge not, and mark but this:
Eternal pit and impassivity, inert
And lasting as the lime of death:
Dissemblings and assemblings of old dross.

Now go, old doll, old heartbox of my pain!
We're victims of our creativity.
Energy spends, the pocket is empty.
The soul must know itself and that is all—
O season between season!—place, an unknown
Destitution, time, a rigor mortis—know

O dispossession! its own emptiness,
The stony image of its lifelessness.

Spirit but plays on matter like blue fire
That darts its tongue above the mass of coals:
Spirit but plays and soon is playéd out
Nothing remains but this blank mirror here,
Subject and object, mirror of the mirrored
'Mid solitude that consummates its crime.

Enwalled and foundered now, the critic soul
In desperate labor would augment its span
Yet knows amid what labors it is found—
Self-help delusions to redress the wound.
What light strike, burn, divorce and fell?
Now ramify your chambers, oh my god!

How weary, cold, unreal, the heats of love,
Exuberance of the senses, fictive lie!
You who are about to die, why should I dare?
I who have died already, how can I?
But stand with empty hands before the Cause
Knowing what wastes and cargoes of my life
Defeat the substance and reduce the will
Complete the mockery and slowly kill.

So come you rest, and abstract me the more
Till strength is gone and paradox'd flesh
Subtract from knower and known, I am
Center of willessness, archaic flame
Unselved and selfless like the turgid stone
In whom time makes its arrogant, cold stand.
Love is the ray that strikes through the blind eye
But ray the eye imagines in its pain

And when the eye is weary, goes the ray again,
Back to the nothingness of the pure mind.
Elegy: mourning, grief and tribute say:
Love must be denied before it's known,
Condemned before it's uttered and despaired
Soon as it's felt: admonisher of ego
It must crack: too weak against the burning
Sun: too close for the all-restless wind, too

Visible for the invisible dark that comes
Alive with promises and possibles
And visions of the angel of the cloud.
Too earthless for the demon of the blood:
In distraction sensual, but in having, slight
Against the august radiance of its origin.

O irony concealed in this harrangue!
The center of no wish is all our hope,
Mere longing for the limits of despair,
Extinction of the hope we can't endure
Where Absolutes outside of time, compute
With their pure fixities, our desperate shifts
And for perfection in those sterile wastes
That death th' ambitious soul must progress to.
Now plunges through my sight residual steel!

VIII

SOME FROM

THIRTY-SIX POEMS AND

A FEW SONGS

From Venice Was That Afternoon

FROM Venice was that afternoon
Though it was our land's canal we viewed.
There willows clove the bluish heat
By dropping leaf or two, gold green
And every tuft of hill beyond
Stood bright, distinct, as if preserved
By glass that sealed out light but not
Its gold or influence.
And floated on the speckled stream
A child of brilliant innocence
Where on the docks of green we stood
Naming it Love for its perfection.
This seemed to be . . .
But the current carried the leaves swiftly,
So flowed that child away from us,
So stared we sternly at the water's empty face.
Ah, in the greenhouse of that hour
Waited in the tare and sorrel
The mouth of fleshliness that stopped:
The leaves that dappled on that breast
The five-sensed image of our pleasance
Have now destroyed its lineaments.
For the waters of that afternoon
Flowed through Negation's glassy land,
Where in this civil, gate-closed hour
The verges of those waters now
Drown that joy that was our power.
What tyranny imposed this pride
That caused love's gift to be denied
And our destroying features to

Cast perpetually on its brow
The glass accepting no leaves now?
In rages of the intellect
We gave to heaven abstinence
Who said our love must issue from
No cisterns of the ruddy sun
But like the artifice of fountains
Leap from cold, infertile sources.
And our destroying features thus
Cast from that land its beingness
And strewed upon the green-fleshed hills
Sands of our darkening great ills.

The Stranger

Now upon this piteous year
I sit in Denmark beside the quai
And nothing that the fishers say
Or the children carrying boats
Can recall me from that place
Where sense and wish departed me
Whose very shores take on
The whiteness of anon.
For I beheld a stranger there
Who moved ahead of me
So tensile and so dancer made
That like a thief I followed her
Though my heart was so alive
I thought myself the equal beauty.
But when at last a turning came
Like the branching of a river
And I saw if she walked on
She would be gone forever,
Fear, then, so wounded me
As fell upon my ear
The voice a blind man dreams
And broke on me the smile
I dreamed as deaf men hear,
I stood there like a spy,
My tongue and eyelids taken
In such necessity.
Now upon this piteous year
The rains of Autumn fall.
Where may she be?
I suffered her to disappear

Who hunger in the prison of my fear.
That lean and brown, that stride,
That cold and melting pride,
For whom the river like a clear,
Melodic line and the distant carrousel
Where lovers on their beasts of play
Rose and fell, that wayfare where the swan adorned
With every wave and eddy
The honor of his sexual beauty,
Create her out of sorrow
That, never perishing,
Is a stately thing.

With Glaze of Tears

WITH glaze of tears or of
Madness, our eyelids winged
The land: tall clouds reflected
Upon us, grass blowing in
Glint of cloud, weird rock, scene of
Our meetings, pathways around
The fen.
Looking into this lucid
Scene flowing beneath us, sight
Dimmed; as if the synapses
Splintered, sight darkened and failed.
For our landscape of love was
Neither each other's features
Since we were each other, but
Rich and violent country.
It was our love's and our
Soul's figuration. Now,
To stand in this separation
From cloud and flower of our kin,
Now in our seeking to close out
All spaces our eyes had run,
To know this land was symbol,
Ethereal, which had fed our veins,
Was ailing of being, was staring
To breathe flower's air or
Flower of us? Confusion trebled.
Leaping and leaping our hearts,
Sight staggered; if landscape was
Different than we, so were we,

So were we, falling, ourselves from
The world cut off, emblem of love
Torn in two.

Theme and Variations

DEAR love, if we're a continent then we,
All strong, deserve its honors too:
Its health and insolence and quaint
Up-building walks, its trees torn down
And wild leaf smell rank as brook beds
And the elve home of owls:
Dear love, if we who meet .are continents
Then have we music, dancing on the needle time,
Whose metrics make an heaven in the mind:
Then have we seasons, trumpeted and strong,
Tongue blessing and the coddler of the eye,
Spool of milkweed, eggs of youngest robins,
The pitted strawberry and the furry snow;
Then have we skies of all countries and folk,
Then be us countries, weather, bells and rock
Then be us bird bone (hollow like a flute)
O oxygen of rose and synthesis
Of root, hate, love and jealousy,
And lechery that fills each sense with revelation.
Then be us each to each
O bubble of the breath of sleep,
O god-borne wing caused by our smiles' meet,
Field, rock and unfelled forest where
Laughing we chide and sleeping bite
And eating dance all hollows of the night
And curry Love who clothes us there
In moon spray and berry, ties us to tides
And laps us, dew and day,
To fairs of such a continent
We are in one another's sight.

Sonnet

NIGHT brings to each the different grudge,
The denser air a taxing of the lung,
The lights that scar, the laughter that is judge
In tavern and in dive when all seems wrong.
To love brings fever and to lust brings food,
To foxes ranging in the dark their luck,
To owls whose ashy claw's their fortitude,
The glittering victim in his patience struck:

Brings potions, cured for some, of rough nightmare,
To some brings plague, like worry to the old,
To some dear mother and the nightcap prayer,
To dogs the fireplace and to sheep the fold,
As brings, as if we'd sleep as if to die,
To each, the dreaded smile of honesty.

The Park

The ceremony of innocence is drowned
Yeats says, and I who cannot understand
Go to the public park to weigh
That elusive and prehensile datum.
Squirrels I meet, eating with their hands,
And pigeons with intoxicated heads,
The violent old like Leonardo's imagery,
The matron, nursemaid and delinquent,
All these detained in duty's ruin I meet.
And in each face that passes me
I look for that ascendant radiance,
The eyes which never turn aside
And belong to others as a tree belongs
To cloud and climate of adjustment.
But each refuses to be seen while all around
The secrets of the plainest bush
Bare their honest reasons to the sun
And bluntest, most enquiring animals.
My will like theirs now halts the quest.
Such privacy has spoiled the heart indeed.
The centre of that fury in which we live
Is confessed by no one but the dead.
Like strangers forced by hate, we greet
Who find no saving faith before the brink
And have plunged down into its boiling dark.

Journey to the Last Station

THAT fish-shaped train, green headed,
Cuts at the rim of distance, which increases:
Still it ingests, the scene it punishes,
Its passage beats the progress of a rose
That's comely eaten and all blown and dark.
Likewise the passage of the night, old cinema
Of years: cars cleaned at Harrisburg:
"Why don't you travel, Bill?" as that old man
Sourly drags the broom through vestibules.
Alone, alone, all confidences left,
The mother station distant on the track,
Statistics lent in exchange but
Formally, as two who play at cards,
Confession, guilt, recrimination checked
As darkness travels to a certain close.
What life, those fields in coils of lava,
Ice eroded, contusions of the snow!
As eyes that fasten on the self's interior
See contours gaping, sequences beheaded,
Till fades, fades, like roses sickening,
Your continuity in robust spring.
Briefest of travelers, you,
Through deserts of the still-life snow,
And clipped by predatory time
Your memory of you as you,
As hurries on the backward wind
The owl-like whistle and the steam
Whose happening but only now you are,
What is but was, the is that fades through you.

The Circle

THE WOOD, swollen with mushrooms,
Those rotting like excrement,
Those blooming in monkey scarlet,
Branch-brown and butter-yellow,
The wood, swollen with voices,
Those high-blood, tortured sexual cries,
The penitential voice singing,
The wood, branch-brown, branched with weeping:

Who am I, am I,
Where the mirror has splashed its bloodless blood,
Who am I in the bloodless wood?
I said: eternity is this:
The formless past within the glass,
The flesh deprived of its true lust,
The inward virtue of the flesh
Corroded by the formless past,
I said: damnnation is this eternity,
The mind divorced at last from act,
Distracted senses caged now judged,
Those thumping ranters damned who drag
The battered actor through such mire,
The act full-judged but not altered
(The crooked blood cannot run straight)
Perversity steals the old color
And red runs white in secret ill.

I said: eternity is this travel
Around and round the center of the wood,
Beset by cries, the sullied pool,

The light of mushrooms, moths running
As large as mice on the forest floor,
The flesh, that battered animal,
Asserting its ample sty has dignity.
I said: eternity devours the mind,
Devours and cannot change by its devouring,
The outward terror remains the same,
And the wood, swollen with mushrooms, the dark wood.

Is Too Late Never

Is TOO late never, are we then to woo
Dear chance forever and the subject late?
Too late my recognition of your worth,
O house behind the cold and punctual gate
I'll never now find entrance to
Whose meaning now I've found too late
I want and only it and only you.

Is too late now the proverb's scalding gibe
As after-knowledge digs its worm-house here?
I revealed every chance to throng
Hardship round you, mock and injure,
Gambled what you gave, joy's bribe,
Nor felt my guilt nor felt love's fear,
Your pain best friend of joy's presumptuous tribe.

Has chance declared the option's ended now,
Repentance may not lease your trust again?
Dead is too late, as when a war's declared
Banished the good queen's golden reign.
Chance gives choice and then lops off the bough.
We're landed with the probable's disdain
In rout of chaos and the splintered vow.

Now is this so, my chances all gone by?
And consequence the coin of all my crime?
(I need not question, for I know what's so
O rhetoric that clangs the old, old chime!)
Cold change has come, dissolving like quicklime
What now endears you like finality.
Repentance is the way we learn to die.

Forest

THERE is the star bloom of the moss
And the hairy chunks of light between the conifers;
There are alleys of light as well where the green leads to
    a funeral
Down the false floor of needles.
There are rocks and boulders that jut, saw-toothed and
    urine-yellow.
Other stones in a field look in the distance like sheep
    grazing,
Grey trunk and trunklike legs and lowered head.
There are short-stemmed forests so close to the ground
You would pity a dog lost there in the spore-budding
Blackness where the sun has never struck down.
There are dying ferns that glow like a gold mine
And weeds and sumac extend the Sodom of color.
Among the divisions of stone and the fissures of branch
Lurk the abashed resentments of the ego.
Do not say this is pleasurable!
Bats, skittering on wires over the lake,
And the bug on the water, bristling in light as he
    measures forward his leaps,
The hills holding back the sun by their notched edges
(What volcanoes lie on the other side
Of heat, light, burning up even the angels)
And the mirrors of forests and hills drawing nearer
Till the lake is all forests and hills made double,
Do not say this is kindly, convenient,
Warms the hands, crosses the senses with promise,
Harries our fear.
Uneasy, we bellow back at the tree frogs

And, night approaching like the entrance of a tunnel,
We would turn back and cannot, we
Surprise our natures; the woods lock us up
In the secret crimes of our intent.

The Brook

THE BROOK contains its landing under water.
There each leaf above is thus
Engrossed by shadow under
Nor there the stone can cleave
Nor filaments that make the structure.
There hang harebell's noise
Blue-peaked, and strung moss.
All is underneath the brook-
Face, a building made by shadow,
An architecture of the seen
As on earth, not under so.
Those shades are most substantial,
Closing out the fish whose plumes
Would make beautiful,
And the sandy minnow.
But as the ambitious fly must go
Into the spider's castle
To be preservéd there
Until the castle's center
Moves upon the venturer,
So I dreamed in my buried wish
My naked senses went
That underwater's cold grandeur.
I dreamed in that most glassy web
I touched with woven breast
Those galleries of glass,
Feeding invisibly on life
As insects use the membrane of the water.

Waking, I Always Waked You Awake

WAKING, I always waked you awake
As always I fell from the ledge of your arms
Into the soft sand and silt of sleep
Permitted by you awake, with your arms firm.

Waking, always I waked immediately
To the face you were when I was off sleeping,
A deer or a swan in a bridal door
Or the ivy looped in the head of a faun.

Waking, always waked to the tasting of dew
As if my sleep issued tears for its loving,
Waking, always waked, swimming from foam,
Breathing from mountains like clad in a cloud,

As waking, always waked in the health of your eyes,
Curled your leaf hair, uncovered your hands,
Good morning like birds in an innocence
Wild as the Indies we ever first found.

The Mouse

WHEN the mouse died at night
He was all overgrown with delight,
His whiskers thick as a wood
From exploring the Polar cupboard
And his eyes still agape
From risky accomplishment.
No honor or drum was his bait.
The more glorious, he
Who with no shame for time
Then boldly died,
Three weeks a rich spell
Of sound and pure smell
And all his long leisure
For meat of short measure
(An ant could carry it.)
Praise him who sweetens
On a small hate.

For All My Friends

THE MOON has thinned; endurance wears it down;
And I must wait until it swells again
And my heart flare, full as that light
Which generates no thing, and burn
When I have brought my friends around,
All caution mocked and futures owned.

So long a living in the savage skull
Accustoms me to no companionable thing
But beasts whose holy certitude walks forth
Like Daniel from his den: my shame, shame.
Yet when I meet those comrades of my choice
All doubt that sued the Vatican

And emptiness inhabiting ambition
Will blush; for there's a marrow in the heart
That only lives by interchange of speech.
As what belief has being in the tomb?
Take mirror away and objectivity,
The hermit is a monster in God's mind.

The shrunken moon now mimics in my room.
I dramatize my patience till the time
When common speech may purify
That moon against the wrinkled pane
And image of the waiting tomb defy
As lions did love Daniel in his doom.

IX

TRIAL AND SAMPLE

Mystic Fit on January 1st

WHAT perfection ran to me
That rain-bound, rain-dark day
That there, dark in that hungering year,
The dark of rain encircled me?
It was the edict that brought me there
To seek the essences that willed me.

Then was it white rain beat
And rendered to us straight
The grave impossibility of all our state?
Unsheltered in the white attack,
Time driving on us all our lack
And building round us wind and fire
To bear to us the fundamental woe
That, being what we were, we chose too much
What, born of the destruction of all else,
Must end, itself, on some destructive truth
As rocks that change the sea must wreck all ships?

Torrential on the icy earth
It wrapped its winding sheet of truth
Wild around us, white and terse.
This was the natural state of want,
This was, exposed, the impulse of our hope,
The bare, dynamic motion of our lives!
O, like the leaves tormented by winter
Blown, flapping, like old blinds against the branch,
Or like the birds seized, battered 'gainst
By strangling winds the serpent-headed cliffs,

What exile, pain, so terrorized us then!
Compound of strait-jackets of rain,
Peaks vanquished us, they lured
With white, improbable pain
And told with obdurate order what,
We, dissoluble with dark, were not
As, wild with different angers, rain
Gashed the cloud and beat the head.

But when taxed, when driven most,
One seizes, as if dying,
On the irrefutable, outflying
What cannot stay a heart so near to death.
The any less than this is not.
Is flawed the crystal at its root.
At all to be simplified,
The heart must be blessed.

O, as runs the soldier through the weirs of death
To go to lie in loathsome stealth,
Black negation, rabid and devouring,
And cries out then the blind wild worth of life,
The instant action, heat and strife,
O as burns he then with woe,
Woe and love, the burning fire,

We wept to weep as if
The *is* confronting what *can't be*
Had mighty curatives within,
As if it were the purest draught,
The starkest sedative of soberness,
Whose very coldness, vigor, bitterness,
Became a wine or portent in the blood

Till knowledge of knowledges seemed possible,
Knowledge to outface the peak with fire.

Who weeps to think we were
Who kneels to know we are,
Who dances, weeps and sings
With nothing to intoxicate the sight
But helpless knowledge that are all,
Brings outward from despair
A joy he may endure,
Impart, impute, to that brute pump
Whose purpose for its clang and shut
And fierce residuum in the dark
Not knowable, is just, and is
Instinctual ecstasy, we pray!

Essay Upon the Collocation of Stones, Shells, Myths, Statues and Dreams

THE SUN arranges to revest the heart
In joy and every animal-headed grief.
The sun unfrocks the buildings in morning.
Likewise it's tender and concise
Although it'd pummel roofs right in.
Now I am what the sun shines on
And am that mangy grass where pigeons stand,
Half-cocked but stalwart in their winter clothes.

A rain has come to sever like a knife
Me from the infancies of holidays
And it has washed swart shells away
And rid the coast of staring bones.
And what of Daphne's eyes already webbed,
Her breasts already hidden, as her thighs
Already bear the leaf that flourishes
To blazon selves across her center's woe?
If we, like Daphne, fleeing lustful gods,
Are changed in dreams to something more than they,
So cheat the chase but not the swaggering god
Have we our lust in metamorphosis?

Sometimes cocks crowing in the nymphal lapse
Between the tides when dying persons die
(A rural cock pent in a city yard
All languishing upon a broken fence!)
Repeat the nuptial miracle I saw:
A hummingbird above the city tops
Who staggered not against the chimney pots!

I say if city cock and he
Wed blights which brought them to the black city
They'll mix their freakishness with honey found
Amid the crisp, enbalming dew of forests pathless
In their enviable prime!

Our muse is never absent but is here
Similar as that marsh straw,
That heavy, golden reek of salty stalk
That hides the clams who've foundered in its roots,
A natural harbor for an as-if-Venus
As if our Muse were all and nothingness,
So came in Protean manners of the hour
To seize our humors with a wizened smile
And be what thought has buried beneath the eyes.
So, if the water that's not blue in particles
But pale and neutral, clings so to her breasts
Like tunics of the spray of wild woodberries
The sight is not incongruous with
The commerce-ploughed, the rusty, veined
And scabrous port of the Sound.

'Whose Muse is now a-whoring at the Wars'?
Mine's here, to recommend great lofts to me
And shores that session magic from the sea.
So as the shell is dyed its blue by the blue sea,
A music grows to coil enchantment round the horn
As Daphne, she, found honor not in laurel
But only from her hands the sprouting leaves
When glazed the eye beheld the prisoned form
And conjugating leaf upon the hand.
In dreams we dream is this a dream?

And suddenly the sea doves start
To cut and quarrel the air between themselves
In leaden capriole, in gigue and caracole,
Blue-edged their wings and in their beaks
The shell they cannot crack on rocks.

And cypress rain has come to bury me.
I'm what no sun is in the simple day
Nor morning's systematic courtesies
Renew the Mozart which was rigor,
Whose phrases sprang as vigorously as arches,
And bridges 'gainst a horned blue sea
Cast up their backs against the glitter's flood.

Nor breakfast now no more in Roman towels
The favorites of the Lord that sweetly sang.